Mubãhala

(Colourful Children's Version)

By

R Mughal

Copyright © 2019 R Mughal
Fourteen Five Limited
All rights reserved.

ISBN-13: 978-1916416161

FOURTEEN FIVE BOOKS
COLOURFUL ISLAMIC NARRATIONS FOR LITTLE MONSTERS

Dedication

"The first person to enter Paradise is Fatimah"

- The Holy Prophet, Muhammed.

I dedicate this book to Fatimah Zahra,

the daughter of Prophet Muhammed.

I pray this humble contribution will

earn me the honour of her intercession.

Acknowledgements

All praise is for Almighty God, without his providence nothing can be conceived or achieved. Thank you to everyone who played an active part in supporting this venture.

Our sincere Thanks to everyone who are supporting us through our social media channels. We held a five-letter word competition; a word that means something to you. The winning word was "Truth" contribute by Mustafa Al-Saadi, from Milton Keynes, United Kingdom.

We selected five more words, Allah, Mahdi, Mercy, Overt and Ya Ali, to help us write a poem as a tribute to our social media family. Our sincere gratitude to everyone that entered, and here are the 12 winners of the additional five words selected:

Sana Ali (Sindh, Pakistan)	Lulu Bafagih (Indonesia)
Nida Fatima (Delhi, India)	Nazar Fatma (Mumbai, India)
Alena Hyder (Karachi, Pakistan)	Azra Hassanali (London, United Kingdom)
Shabana Kalyan (Mombasa, Kenya)	Dilshad Merchant (London, United Kingdom)
T.K Richards (Charleston, SC, USA)	Maryam Salim (Dar-e-Salaam, Tanzania)
Samar Sayed (Mumbai, India)	@syeda.zaineb

"Truth"

Out of the night that covers us,

Infinite the clay pit from where we emerged.

I thank Allah for delivering a Truth

For us, discretional creatures still submerged.

The Truth has always existed

Not bound by space or time.

Why question it now?

Because 'we' exist? and ponder "how?"

The Truth was never chance,

Nor it came about of circumstance.

It exists amongst grief and tears

Yet fortifies its space everywhere.

Standing tall, overt, unafraid

Divine providence declares them, Ahlul Bayt.

The rope of mercy strides, Ya Ali to Mahdi,

"Ali is with the Truth, and the Truth is with Ali."

As menacing are, those darkest times

The devil cannot imitate pious bloodlines.

A fighting chance to stand and deliver,

Let not your voice shake or quiver.

Uttering the Truth aligns your fate,

Striding with fervour alongside our Ahlul Bayt.

Minority they may stay, but Truth is justice

And Truth; unfailingly prevails.

R Mughal

(Author)

The Prophet Muhammad has a daughter;

Her name is Fatima Zahra.

Can you remember her from the Event of the Kisa?

The Kisa illuminated the Ahlul Bayt.

What personalities,

what wonderful traits!

Here's another event the Prophet wishes to mention;

It's called Mubāhala.

"When did it happen?" I hear you question.

On the 24th day, of the month of Dhul-Hijjah.

One bright starry night as the angels gathered, Muhammad asked Ali to write some letters. His pen was rather special, made of one tall silky feather.

Muhammed posted the letters to faraway places, wishing to pass on knowledge about Allah's good graces.

A little while later, Muhammad received a reply.

It came from Najran in Yemen,

a place not nearby.

It was from Abu Haritha, a grand Christian priest.

Muhammad wondered when they would meet.

Abu Haritha also pondered,

    "What's it like to meet a Prophet of God?"

When he was a little boy,

    Abu Haritha learned about Jesus.

He learned Jesus was an almighty lord.

But Muhammad said, "Jesus is a prophet,

    a Messenger of God."

A few weeks later, Abu Haritha arrived,
   with friends in tow.

They were all surprised!

How humble was the Prophet,
   standing with Ali.

How gracious and noble was this family!

"Who is your Lord?" started Abu Haritha.

"There can only be One," replied Muhammad.

"His name is Allah,

and I am his Prophet."

The questions kept coming,

to and fro.

Abu Haritha started to learn,

Jesus was <u>not</u> an almighty lord.

Allah the Almighty Lord had a plan,
His precious words are recorded in the Qur'an
(3:61)

فَمَنْ حَاجَّكَ فِيهِ مِن بَعْدِ مَا جَاءَكَ مِنَ الْعِلْمِ فَقُلْ تَعَالَوْا نَدْعُ أَبْنَاءَنَا وَأَبْنَاءَكُمْ وَنِسَاءَنَا وَنِسَاءَكُمْ وَأَنفُسَنَا وَأَنفُسَكُمْ ثُمَّ نَبْتَهِلْ فَنَجْعَل لَّعْنَتَ اللَّـهِ عَلَى الْكَاذِبِينَ

'Should anyone argue with you concerning him, after the knowledge that has come to you, say, 'Come! Let us call our sons and your sons, our women and your women, our souls and your souls, then let us pray earnestly, and call down Allah's wrath upon the liars.' (3:61)

(Translated by 'Qarai' Tanzil.net)

Allah set a competition, for which He said,

"Bring your children, your women, and yourselves."

Allah would be happy with the truthful ones,

    and not so pleased with the troublesome ones.

It was getting dark and nearly time for bed.

    Muhammad was not tired, his mind thinking ahead.

Straight away he knew who to bring

    to the competition, so they could win.

The competition was Allah's graceful design,

    for Abu Haritha to learn, to strive, and accept truthful ways.

For Abu Haritha to know about us—the Ahlul Bayt.

The competition day had finally arrived, the day of Mubāhala.

Salman Farsi came to Muhammad, and said "Subhan'Allah."

With a smile Salman helped to tidy the place up. Rolling out the red carpet for the Ahlul Bayt to walk on.

The sun was shining, a wonderful start.

People had gathered from near and far.

The grand priest arrived with his folk,

    and Muhammad with his Ahlul Bayt calmly approached.

Excitement and glee filled the air,
  people chattering everywhere.
Suddenly, from the crowd,
  a priest with Abu Haritha asked aloud.

"Who are these people walking with Muhammad?"

A single voice from the crowd replied,

  "This is Ali, Fatimah, Hassan and Hussayn.
  His cousin, his daughter, and the two young
  Successors of his reign."

"We are ready," said the Ahlul Bayt.

But Abu Haritha looked quite dismayed!

His folk all seemed quite surprised,

to see there were only...FIVE!

"Wait," he shouted back and looked up at the sky.

The clouds looked dark, and not so very nice.

"We need a moment to think," he cried.

Everyone nodded their heads by his side.

A moment of truth settled on Abu Haritha and his folk.

He saw a kind family facing his hundreds and more.

"I would only bring my family if I knew the truth," he whispered.

"Muhammad must be a Prophet."

They all nodded and listened.

Abu Haritha approached Muhammad.

He spoke softly and his voice was humbled.

"O Muhammad, we will not enter this Mubāhala,

we know you are a Prophet of Allah.

We want to live peacefully and happily,

and not disappoint the Almighty."

Abu Haritha addressed the crowd,

"Listen, everyone!

The faces of the Ahlul Bayt are like the glowing sun.

If they asked Allah to squash a huge mountain,

    Allah would do it without hesitation!"

People gathered in the crowd could see,

    Allah loved the Ahlul Bayt dearly.

The dark clouds had scurried away,

    and the warm sun shone brightly again.

The crowd jumped up and cheered loudly,

"Hurray!" they resounded, looking on so proudly.

The Ahlul Bayt has won!

A day of celebration!

Eid-e-Mubāhala will never be forgotten.

Extra notes:

The significance of the event of Mubāhala

In responding to Allah's command, the Prophet (s.a.w) brought with him, Imam Hasan (a.s) and Imam Hussayn (a.s), because they were the sons of his daughter Fatimah Zahra (a.s), and for this, they are his sons. He brought Fatimah Zahra (a.s) with him because she represents the women from the members of his Household.

Bringing Imam 'Ali (a.s) with him indicates that the Messenger of God considered Imam Ali (a.s) an extension of his personality. By considering him so, he elevated him above all the Muslims.

The Messenger (s.a.w) said on many occasions: "'Ali is from me and I am from him."

Why the Event is considered a day of Celebration, Eid:

- The event proved to be an end of a power struggle between all faiths (including Muslims who were picking and choosing elements of the faith) questioning the authenticity of the words of Allah and the Holy Prophet (S.A.W).

- The invitation of 'Mubāhala' was directed by Allah, and it was in compliance with His Command that the Holy Prophet (s.a.w) took his Ahlul Bayt (a.s) along with him.

  This shows how affairs relating to Prophethood and the religion of God are determined by the Will of God; allowing no interference from the common people (Ummah). The matter of Imam Ali's (a.s) succession followed by eleven Imams to the office of religious leaders should be viewed in this perspective.

- The status of 'Ali, Fatimah, Hasan and Hussayn in following the directions of the Holy Prophet (s.a.w) could no longer be disputed. This event established who the members of the Prophet's household (Ahlul-Bayt) (a.s) were, and their spiritual purity.

- Despite their childhood, Imam Hasan (a.s) and Imam Hussayn (a.s) served as the active partners of the Holy Prophet (s.a.w) in the event of Mubāhala. This yields the conclusion that age is no criteria for the greatness of the infallibles (Ma'sumeen). They are born adorned with virtues and knowledge.

- The Holy Prophet's (s.a.w) act of having preferred a few (Quality over Quantity) further elevates their status above all others.

We pray for the success of all our young readers!

@FourteenFiveBooks

Check out our Hadith Al Kisa book titles!

English
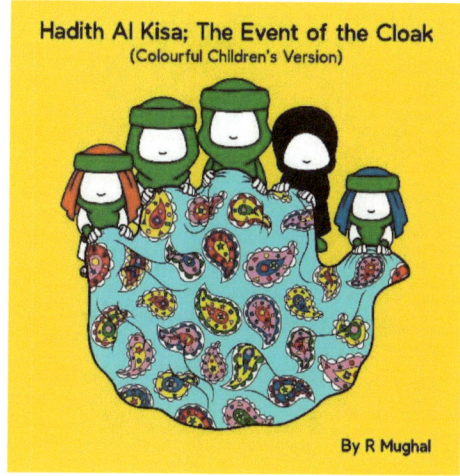

Farsi
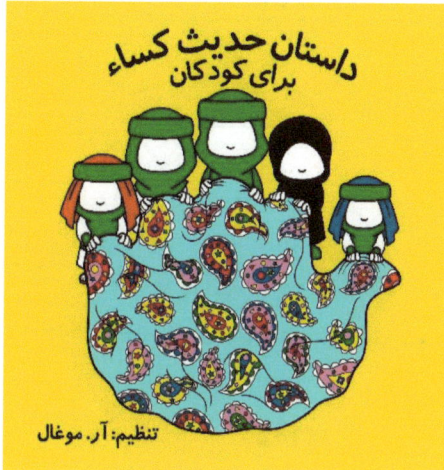

Danish

Ordering Information for all our books

USA, Canada, UK, Germany, France, Italy, Netherlands, Japan, India, Brazil, Mexico, Australia

 FOURTEEN FIVE BOOKS

www.FourteenFiveBooks.co.uk

www.ingramcontent.com/pod-product-compliance
Lightning Source LLC
Chambersburg PA
CBHW042122040426
42450CB00002B/44